Back to Basics™

YEARS 2 & 3

MULTIPLICATION TABLES

Do you need to know the basics of multiplication tables? Let's learn about them together.

Parents and carers are encouraged to read the explanation and practice sections with their child.

Ann Baker

Illustrated by
Janice Bowles

About this book

Each unit in this book begins with a brief **explanation** of a concept or a strategy. You are encouraged to read this explanation with your child and, where appropriate, to use everyday materials and examples to give meaning to the concepts.

We practise is a worked example for you and your child to discuss together, paying particular attention to the thinking processes required to understand the concept or apply the strategy.

You practise gives your child the opportunity to practise the concept or strategy. It also indicates how well your child understands the new material and often includes problem-solving questions to ensure that your child has mastered the concept or strategy.

If further support is required, you and your child's teacher can devise a plan to ensure that all the basic concepts are fully understood and consolidated.

The **Tests** at the end of the book are provided to check that the concepts are fully understood. Test 1 can be done after units 1–10 are completed and Test 2 when the book is finished.

Meet 'BOB' – Back Of the Book

At the end of each unit, BOB reminds your child to go to the Answers section at the back of the book.

Mathematical Content

This book has been designed to cover the concept of multiplication tables that your child will encounter in **Year 2** and **Year 3**. It also revises some concepts from **Year 1**. The units provide a comprehensive coverage of the following Key Topics from the **Australian Curriculum: Mathematics.**

Australian Curriculum : Mathematics

YEAR 1

Skip count by twos, fives and tens starting from zero (ACMNA012)

YEAR 2

Investigate number sequences, initially those increasing and decreasing by twos, threes, fives and ten from any starting point and moving to other sequences (ACMNA026)

Recognise and represent multiplication as repeated addition, groups and arrays (ACMNA031)

Recognise and represent division as grouping into equal sets and solve problems using these representations (ACMNA032)

Recognise and interpret common uses of halves, quarters and eighths of shapes and collections (AMNA033)

YEAR 3

Recall multiplication facts to two, three, five and ten and related division facts (ACMNA056)

Represent and solve problems involving multiplication using efficient mental and written strategies and appropriate digital technologies (ACMNA057)

Contents & Checklist

WRITING and TALKING ABOUT MULTIPLICATION TABLES

When you combine **two groups of three**, you can say it as:

2 times 3   2 lots of 3   2 multiplied by 3   double 3

Whichever way you say it, the answer is 6.

This **multiplication fact** is written as: **2 × 3 = 6**

The cross × is a **multiplication** sign. When you see this sign you can use **multiplication tables** (times tables) to find the answer.

Look at this picture of **2 plates with 5 cherries** on each.

You can write this as: 2 × 5 = 10

Now look at this picture of **5 plates with 2 cherries** on each.

You can write this as: 5 × 2 = 10

This means that **2 × 5 = 10** can also be written as:

5 × 2 = 10

5 + 5 = 10

2 lots of 5

2 + 2 + 2 + 2 + 2 = 10

5 lots of 2

When multiplying, it doesn't matter if you swap the numbers around.

GAME CARD IDEAS

Cut out the game cards – they will last longer if they are laminated. Here are some games for you to try.

MULTIPLICATION GAME 1

A game for 2 players. Players are dealt six cards each, face-up, and four cards are put in a pool in the middle, also face-up.

Players take turns to try to make a correct multiplication sequence using their own cards. For example, from 4, 2, 6, 8, 0, 3, the 2, 4, 8 or the 2, 3, 6 can make $2 \times 4 = 8$ or $2 \times 3 = 6$. The used cards are set aside and replaced so that both players have six cards for the next round.

If players cannot make a sequence using their cards, they can swap cards from the pool. When all possibilities are exhausted, the player who has made most complete sequences wins the game. As proficiency increases, cards can be held closed.

Multiplication Game 2

A game for 2 players. This game is similar to *Multiplication Game 1*, except that all cards are counted at the end (not sets of cards) and the player with most cards wins.

The important difference is that when a player attempts to make a multiplication sequence with a two-digit answer (rather than one-digit) more cards are used. For example, the cards 2, 3, 6, 1, 2, 5 can generate $2 \times 3 = 6$ or $2 \times 6 = 12$. The latter gets 4 points, so it is better than $2 \times 3 = 6$, which only gets 3 points.

NOTE: Games are meant to be fun and provide practice without stress. It is recommended that you stop playing while you are still having fun and then your child will want to play again another time. Allow use of the multiplication grid in Unit 12 in the early stages.

UNIT 1 COUNTING in 2s

Being able to count in 2s is an important skill.

Look at this **counting sequence**.
You will notice that every second number is **red**.

1	2	3	4	5	6	7	8	9	10
11	12	13	14	15	16	17	18	19	20

The **red** numbers show the **2s counting sequence**.

Read the **red** numbers as fast as you can.
Can you go even faster? Can you go backwards?

Can you say the numbers at the same time as the calculator display? If you practise enough you will be able to.

You can make your **calculator** into a **count-by-2s machine** by pressing these keys:

We practise

Complete this counting-by-2s sequence.

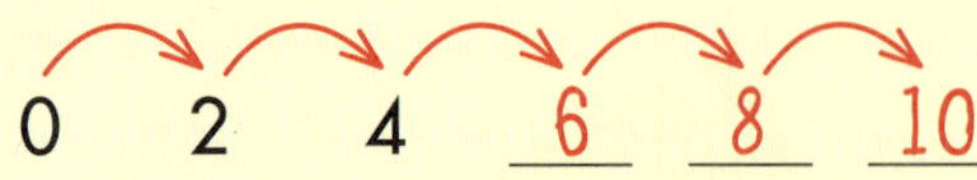

0 2 4 6 8 10

How many jumps of 2 are needed to get from start to finish?

5

Complete this counting sequence to find the starting number and the finishing number.

6 8 10 12 14

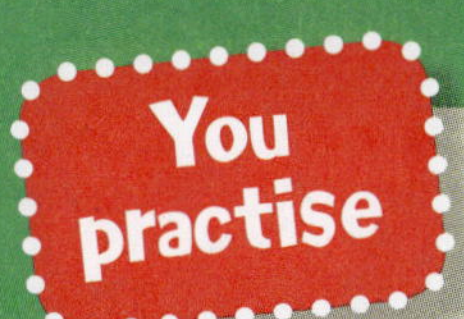

Complete each counting-by-2s sequence. How many jumps of 2 are needed to get from start to finish?

0 2 4 ___ ___ ___ ___

___ jumps

0 2 4 6 ___ ___ ___ ___

___ jumps

Use the **counting-by-2s sequence** on the opposite page if you need to.

0 2 4 6 8 10 ___ ___ ___ ___ ___ ___

___ jumps

20 18 16 ___ ___ ___ ___ ___ ___ ___ ___

___ jumps

You practise

Complete each counting-by-2s sequence.

___ 4 6 8 ___ ___

___ 6 8 10 ___ ___ ___

___ 6 8 10 ___ ___ ___ ___

8

___ ___ 16 ___ ___ ___ ___ ___

BOB time!

SPEED COUNTING in 2s

When you need to count a lot of objects, it can really speed things up if you put them into groups of 2s and then count in 2s.

Count by **1s** to find out how many counters are here.

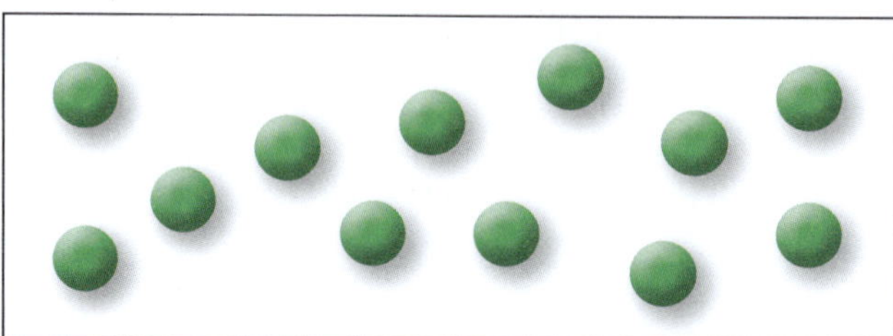

Below is the same number of counters, but they are divided into **groups of 2s**. Count each group of 2 to check how many there are altogether.

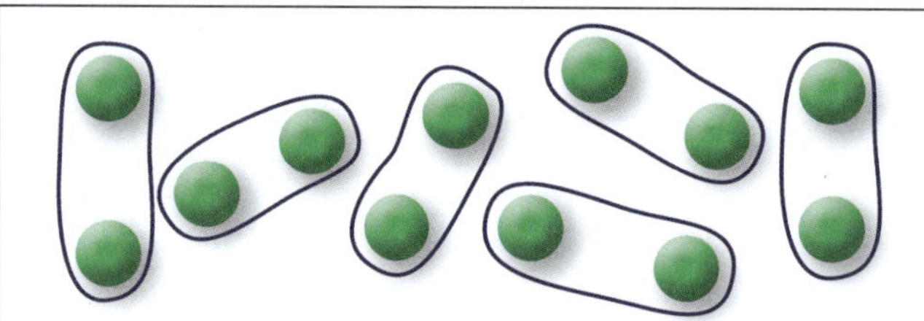

Did you count **6 groups of 2s** and **12** in total?
You can write this as a multiplication fact:

2 × 6 = 12

Did you notice that counting by 2s is a lot faster?

We practise

Count by 2s and complete the multiplication fact.

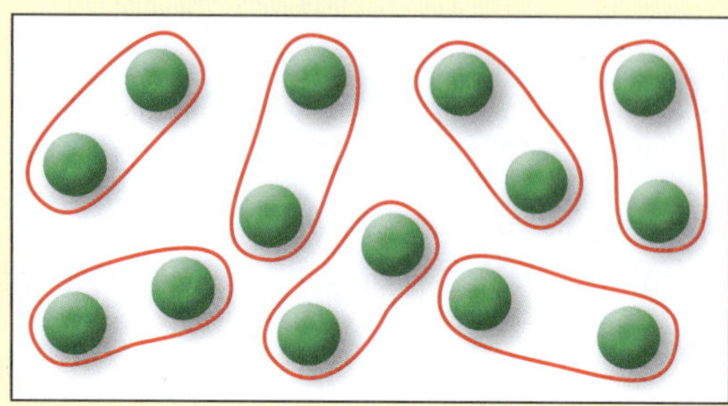

7 × 2 = 14

Draw 16 counters and divide them into groups of 2s. Then complete the multiplication fact.

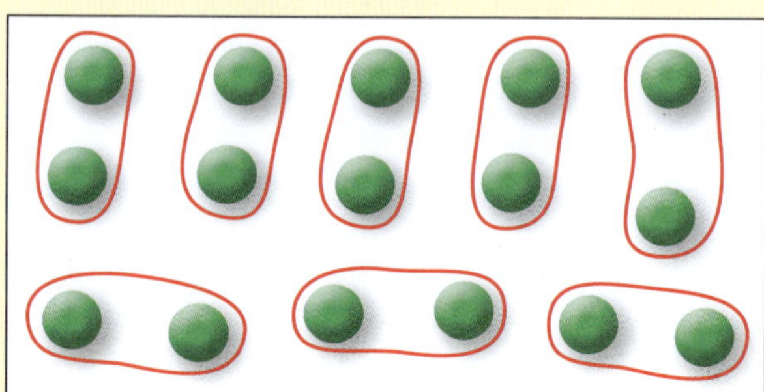

8 × 2 = 16

You practise

Divide the counters into groups of 2s and then count by 2s to complete each multiplication fact.

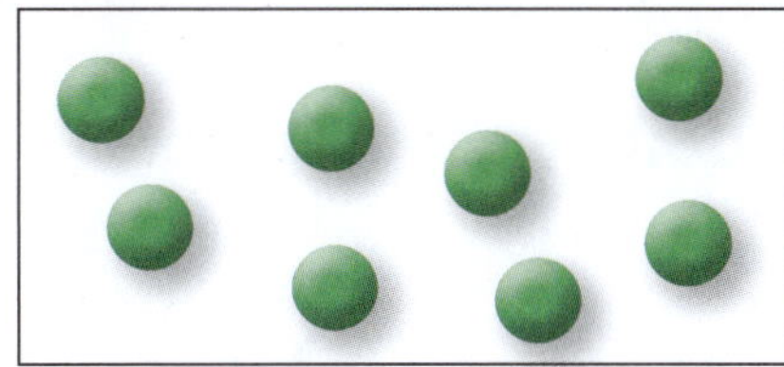

___ × 2 = ____

___ × 2 = ____

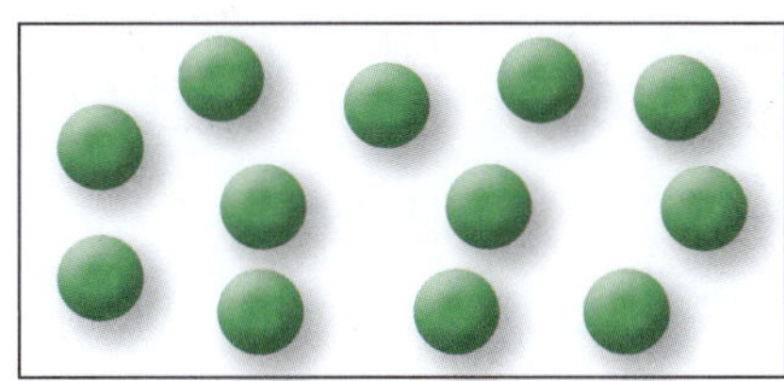

___ × 2 = ____

___ × 2 = ____

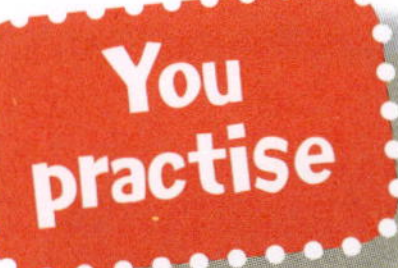

Draw the total number of counters and divide them into groups of 2. Then complete each multiplication fact.

___ × 2 = 10

___ × 2 = 20

___ × 2 = 14

___ × 2 = 22

BOB time!

DOUBLING

If you play dice games, then you already know some doubles.

Double 5 is 10
2 × 5 =10

Double 6 is 12
2 × 6 = 12

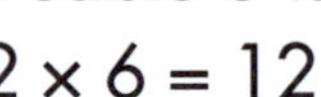

There are doubles everywhere you look.

Look at a spider's legs – **double 4**, which is 8 legs altogether.

Look inside an egg carton – **double 6**, which is 12 eggs altogether.

Did you know that there are **double doubles** as well? Check out these dice.

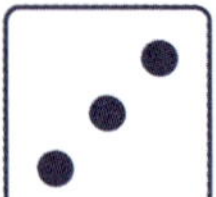 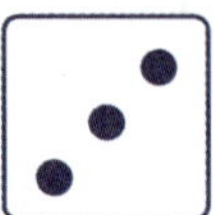 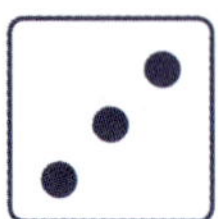 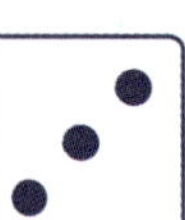

Can you see **double 3** and another **double 3**?

Double 3 is **6**   **2 × 3 = 6**

Double 6 is **12**   **2 × 6 = 12**

Look around you for more doubles.

We practise

What double is shown here? 7

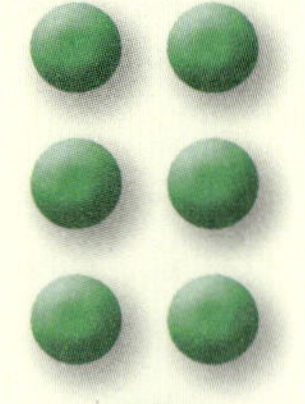 

Complete this double multiplication fact.

Double 7 is 14   2 × 7 = 14

Draw double double 5.

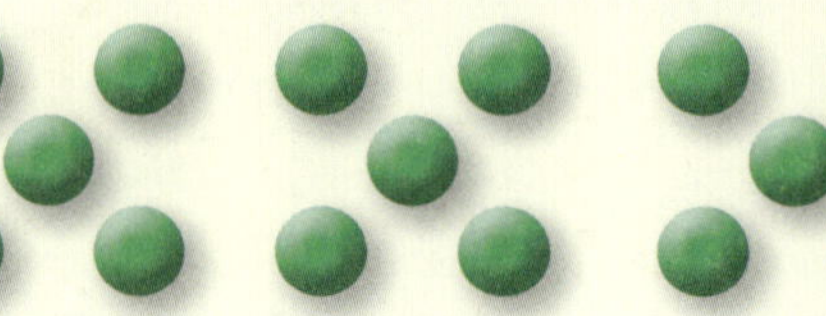

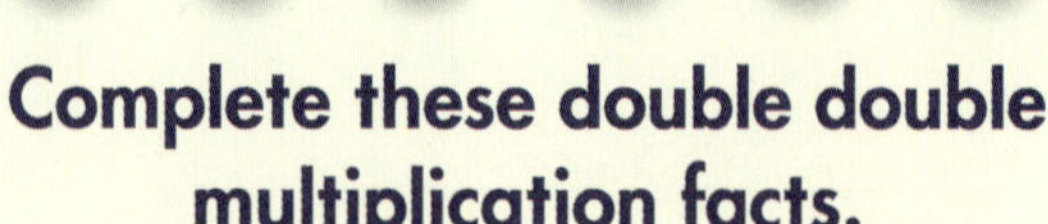

Complete these double double multiplication facts.

Double 5 is 10   2 × 5 = 10

Double 10 is 20   2 × 10 = 20

You practise Find the double and complete each multiplication fact.

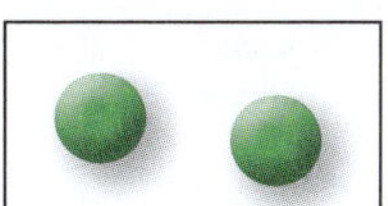 

Double ____ is ____ 2 × ____ = ____

Double ____ is ____ 2 × ____ = ____

Double ____ is ____ 2 × ____ = ____

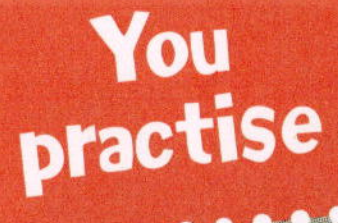

Complete each double double multiplication fact.

  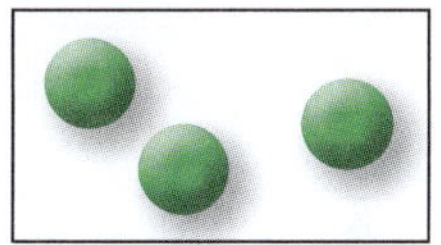 

Double ____ is ____ 2 × ____ = ____

Double ____ is ____ 2 × ____ = ____

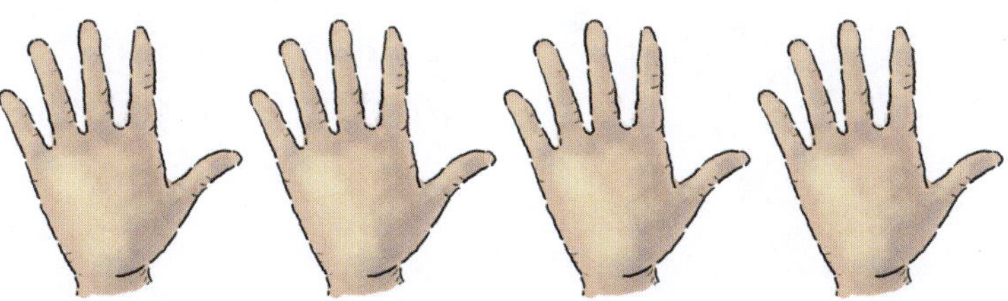

Double ____ is ____ 2 × ____ = ____

Double ____ is ____ 2 × ____ = ____

Double ____ is ____ 2 × ____ = ____

Double ____ is ____ 2 × ____ = ____

BOB time!

COUNTING in 5s

As well as counting in 2s, counting in 5s is also a very important skill.

Look at the coins below.
One quick way to count these coins is to **count in 5s**.

      = 30c

5 10 15 20 25 30

How would you find the total value of these coins?

Look at the table below. You will notice that very fifth number is **red**. This is the **5s counting sequence**.

1	2	3	4	5	6	7	8	9	10
11	12	13	14	15	16	17	18	19	20
21	22	23	24	25	26	27	28	29	30
31	32	33	34	35	36	37	38	39	40

You can make your **calculator** into a **count-by-5s machine** by pressing these keys:

Can you say the numbers at the same time as the calculator display? If you practise enough you will be able to.

We practise

Complete this counting-by-5s sequence.

0 5 10 15 20 25 30

How many jumps of 5 are needed to get from start to finish? 6

Complete this counting sequence to find the starting number and the finishing number.

5 10 15 20 25

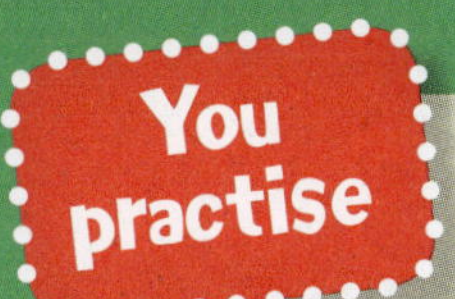

Complete each counting-by-5s sequence. How many jumps are needed to get from start to finish?

1. 0 5 10 ___ ___ ___ ___

___ jumps

Use the **counting-by-5s sequence** on the opposite page if you need to.

2. 0 5 10 15 ___ ___ ___ ___

___ jumps

3. 0 5 10 15 20 25 ___ ___ ___ ___ ___

___ jumps

4. 45 40 35 30 ___ ___ ___ ___ ___ ___

___ jumps

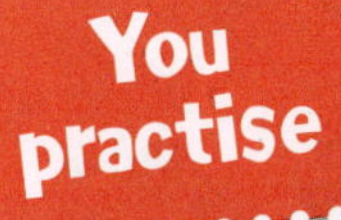

Complete each counting-by-5s sequence.

5. ___ 5 10 15 ___

6. ___ 15 20 25 ___ ___

7. ___ ___ 25 30 35 ___

8. ___ 45 40 35 ___ ___ ___ ___ ___

SPEED COUNTING in 5s

When you need to count a lot of things it can really speed things up if you count in 5s.

Below is a collection of counters that are **divided** into **groups of 5**. Count each group to work out how many there are altogether.

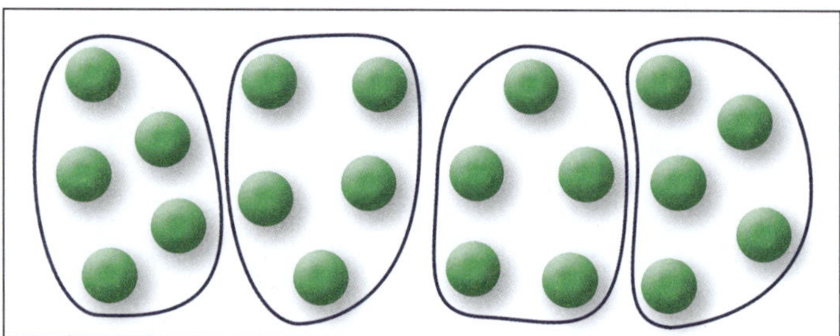

There are **4 groups of 5**, which means that there are **20 counters** altogether.

You can write this as a multiplication fact: **4 × 5 = 20**

A tally is another way of counting in 5s and is a good way to keep score for a game.

Look at this score sheet – each group of tallies has 5 lines.

It is easy to see Ann's score is 6 lots of 5. **6 × 5 = 30**

And Johnny's score is 5 lots of 5.
5 × 5 = 25

You can count by 5s or with practice you will soon just know these multiplication facts.

Score sheet

Ann	Johnny
卌	卌
卌	卌
卌	卌
卌	卌
卌	卌
卌	

We practise

Divide these counters into groups of 5 and count in 5s to complete the multiplication fact.

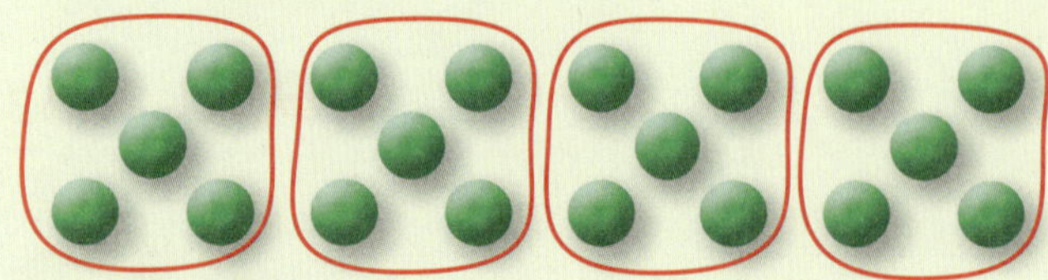

4 × 5 = 20

Draw tallies for 6 × 5 and then finish the multiplication fact.

卌 卌 卌 卌 卌 卌

6 × 5 = 30

You practise

Divide the counters into groups of 5s and count in 5s to complete each multiplication fact.

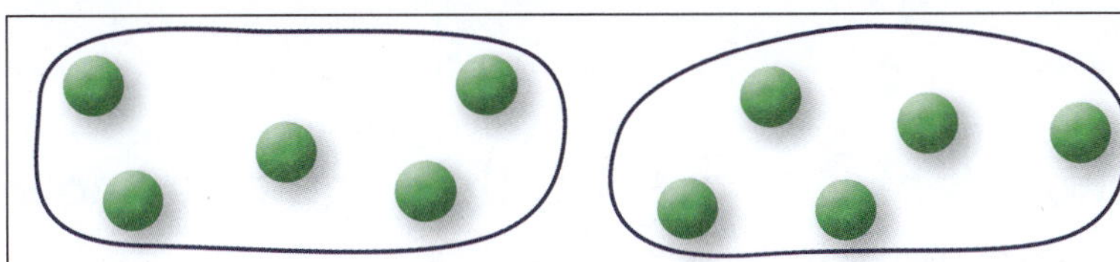

____ × 5 = ______

____ × 5 = ______

____ × 5 = ______

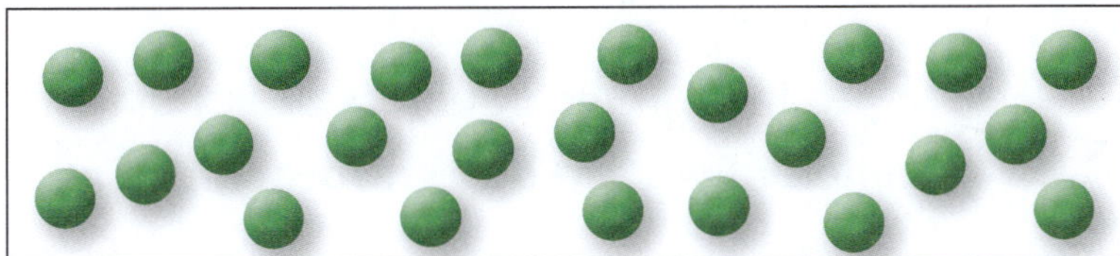

____ × 5 = ______

You practise

Draw tallies and complete each multiplication fact.

7 × 5 = ____

6 × 5 = ____

9 × 5 = ____

8 × 5 = ____

BOB time!

TURNAROUNDS

Good news: **turnarounds** work for all multiplication facts.

If you know that 2 × 6 = 12, then you also know its turnaround, which is 6 × 2 = 12.

That's right, they both have the **same answer**, **12**. And they both use the **same numbers**, but in a **different order**.

Look at this diagram of **2 × 6**.

And look at this diagram of **6 × 2**.

Even though the counters are arranged differently, both have a **total of 12**.

Check these multiplication facts on your calculator.

5 × 3 = ? **3 × 5 = ?**

Yes, they also have the **same answer**.

That's because **3 × 5** is the **turnaround** of **5 × 3**. The same numbers are multiplied, but in a different order.

We practise

Complete these multiplication facts and write their turnarounds.

2 × 8 = 16	5 × 3 = 15
8 × 2 = 16	3 × 5 = 15

You practise Complete each multiplication fact and its turnaround.

 2 × 6 = ____ 6 × 2 = ____

 5 × 4 = ____ 4 × 5 = ____

 2 × 7= ____ 7 × 2 = ____

 2 × 9 = ____ 9 × 2 = ____

 5 × 6 = ____ 6 × 5 = ____

Remember to **count in 2s or 5s** if you get stuck.

You practise Complete each multiplication fact and write the turnaround.

 5 × 4 = ____ ____ × ____ = ____

 2 × 4 = ____ ____ × ____ = ____

 5 × 10 = ____ ____ × ____ = ____

 5 × 7 = ____ ____ × ____ = ____

 2 × 9 = ____ ____ × ____ = ____

BOB time!

10s COUNTING SEQUENCE

The easiest speed counting sequence of them all is the 10s sequence.

One way to work out how much money is here is to **count in 10s** really quickly.

How would you work out **how much money** there is here?

10 20 30 40 50 60 70 80 90 100 = 100c or $1

Did you notice that every number ends with **0** in the **10s** counting sequence?

Look at the 5s counting sequence below.

Did you notice that every number ends with **5** or **0**?

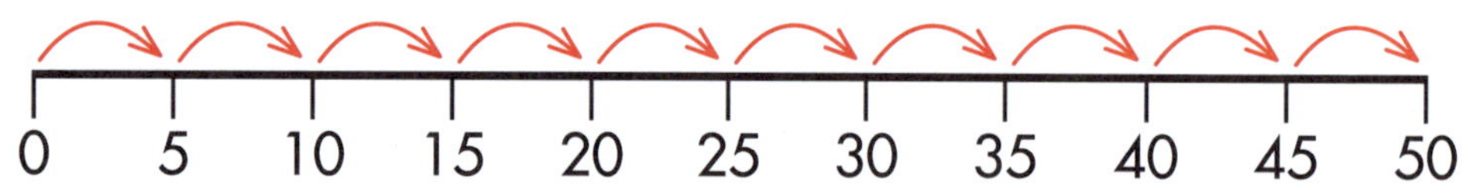

Did you also notice that every number that ends with 0 is in both the 5s and the 10s counting sequences?

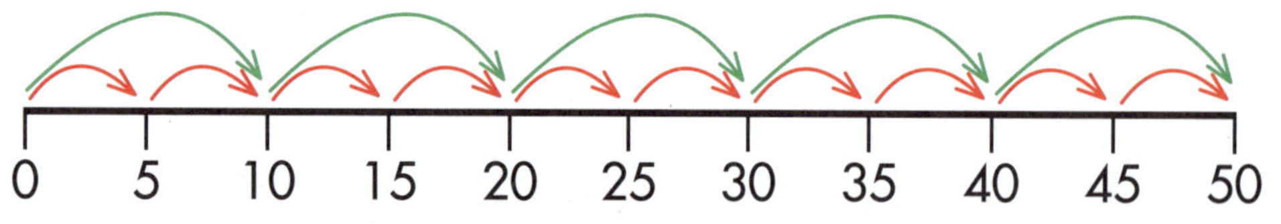

Because 45 ends in 5, it belongs in the 5s sequence. And because 50 ends in 0, it must be in both the 5s and 10s sequence.

We practise

Circle the number that is in the 10s counting sequence.

21 43 35 (80) 45

How many 10s make that number? 8

Circle the number that is in both the 10s and the 5s counting sequence.

13 52 22 (40) 35

How many 5s make that number?
How many 10s make that number?

8 5s 4 10s

You practise Answer each question.

1 Circle the number that is in the 10s counting sequence.
How many 10s are needed to make this number?

33 56 40 ____ 10s

Remember you can **draw a diagram** to help you understand the problem.

2 Circle the number that is in the 5s counting sequence.
How many 5s are needed to make this number?

53 35 26 ____ 5s

3 Circle the numbers that are in both the 10s and the 5s counting sequences.
How many 5s and how many 10s are needed to make each number?

35 46 50 ____ 5s and ____ 10s

43 55 40 ____ 5s and ____ 10s

4 Circle the number that is in 5s, but not in the 10s counting sequence.
How many 5s are needed to make this number?

82 60 45 ____ 5s

Write the multiplication facts for each number.

5 **10** ____ × 5 = ____ ____ × 10 = ____

6 **30** ____ × 5 = ____ ____ × 10 = ____

BOB time!

DON'T BE TRICKED

The multiply by 1 and 0 are the two multiplication tables that sometimes trick people. You can avoid being tricked by understanding what multiply by 1 and multiply by 0 really mean.

Multiplying by 1

3 × 1 means **three groups of 1**.

Some people think the answer to 3 × 1 is 4. No! 4 is the answer to 3 + 1.

3 × 1

1 × 3

Multiplying by 0

Some people think the answer to 3 × 0 is 3. But this can't be correct because if you have 3 lots of nothing, you still have nothing.

How many cherries are on these three plates? None.

See the empty plates. Nothing there! And if there are no plates, then there are no cherries!

3 × 0 = 0 **0 × 3 = 0**

We practise

Write the multiplication fact for this problem.

I have 1 bag with 4 apples in it. How many apples do I have altogether?

1 × 4 = 4

Match each multiplication fact with the correct answer. Circle the answer that does not belong.

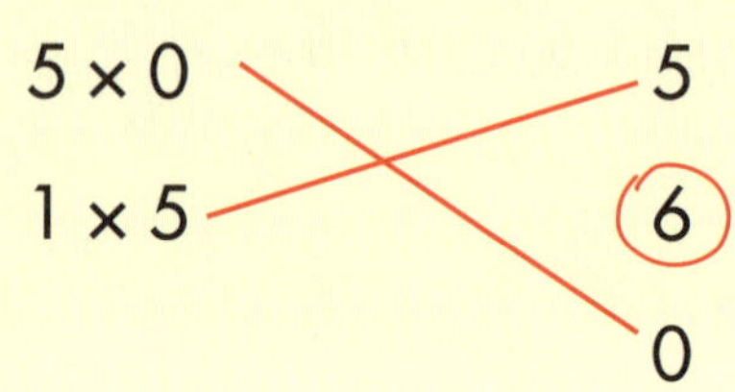

5 × 0	5
1 × 5	(6)
	0

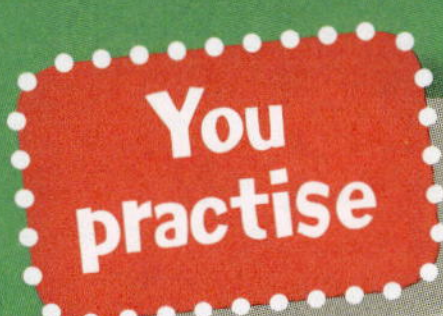

Write the multiplication fact for each problem.

3 plates with 1 apple on each plate

___ × ___ = ___

1 plate with 6 apples on it

___ × ___ = ___

3 plates with 0 apples on each plate

___ × ___ = ___

0 plates with 1 apple on each plate

___ × ___ = ___

Think carefully and don't be tricked!

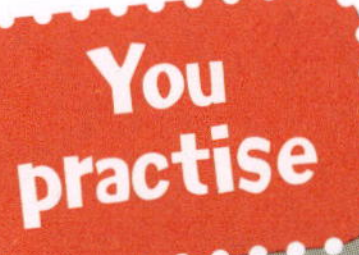

Match each multiplication fact with the correct answer. Circle the answers that do not belong.

	3
0 × 6	4
3 × 1	0
	6

7

	8
0 × 8	7
1 × 6	6
	0

	8
4 × 0	4
1 × 7	7
	0

	8
9 × 0	9
9 × 1	0
	10

BOB time!

MAKING CONNECTIONS

5 + 5 + 5 or 

There are many ways of writing this **multiplication fact**.

3 lots of 5 or **3 × 5**

If you already know 3 × 5 as a **multiplication fact**, then it is **quicker to multiply** than to **add** or **count in 5s**.

Whenever you come across lots of the same number or amounts to add together, ask yourself:

"Can I use a multiplication fact here?"

Look at this example.

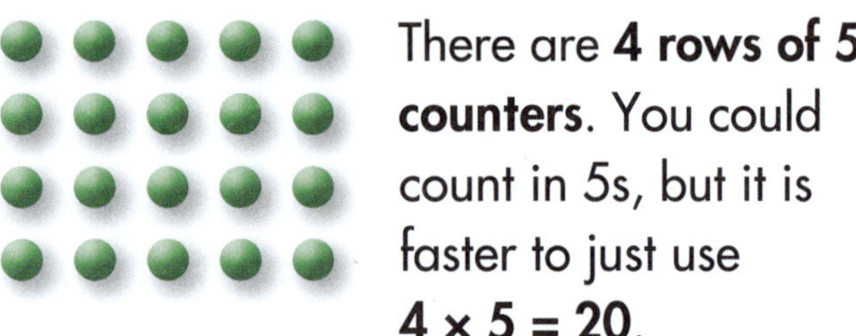

There are **4 rows of 5 counters**. You could count in 5s, but it is faster to just use **4 × 5 = 20**.

If you turn these rows around, you can now see **5 rows of 4 counters**.

You can count these using **5 × 4** or **4 × 5**. Either way the answer is still **20**.

To work out **6 lots of 5 tallies**, you could use **6 × 5**.

We practise

What multiplication fact matches this addition sentence? What is the answer?

2 + 2 + 2 + 2 + 2 + 2 + 2 = 14

7 × 2 = 14

What multiplication fact matches the picture? How many wings altogether?

4 × 2 = 8 wings altogether

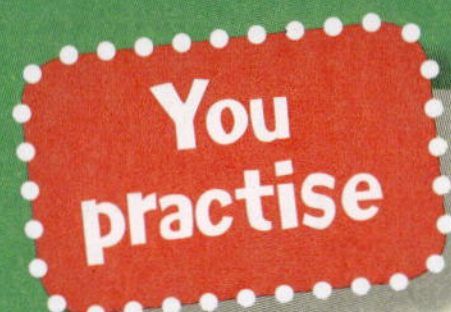

What multiplication fact matches each picture?
How many things altogether in each picture?

___ × ___ = ___

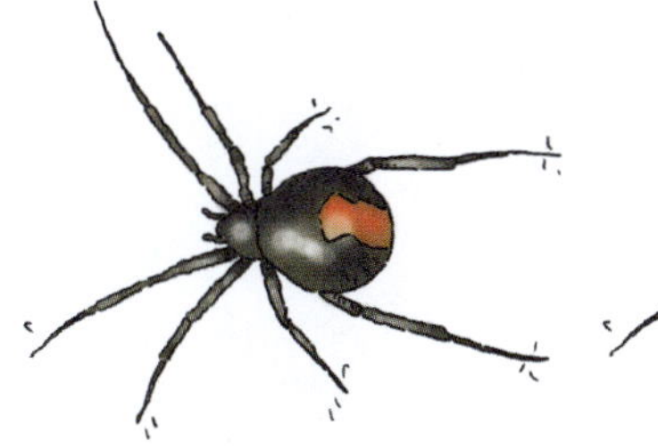 

___ × ___ = ___

𝍸 𝍸 𝍸 𝍸 𝍸 𝍸 𝍸

___ × ___ = ___

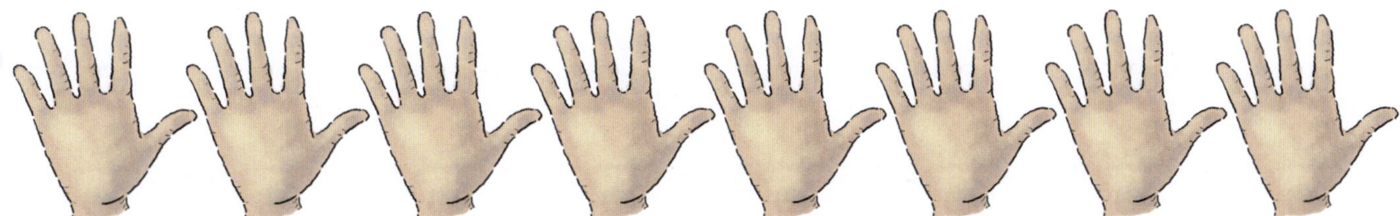

___ × ___ = ___

___ × ___ = ___

𝍸 𝍸 𝍸 𝍸 𝍸

___ × ___ = ___

PROBLEM SOLVING

Clare has made surprise treat bags for 3 of her friends. She has put 5 treats in each bag.

How many treats did Clare use altogether for the treat bags?

Notice that the important information is highlighted in blue and what has to be found out is highlighted in pink.

Drawing a picture of the bags is one way to solve this problem.

= 15 treats altogether

Using an **addition sentence** is another way of solving this problem. **5 + 5 + 5 = 15**

However, if you know your multiplication facts, then **multiplication** is the fastest way. **3 × 5 = 15**

Addition is too slow! Think multiplication.

Highlight the important information and what you have to find out in this problem.

Jake threw five dice. He threw 5, 5, 5, 5 and 5.
What is Jake's score?

Draw a picture to help solve this problem.

     = 25

What addition sentence could you use to solve this problem?

5 + 5 + 5 + 5 + 5 = 25

What multiplication fact could you use to solve this problem?

5 × 5 = 25

You practise

Highlight the important information and solve each problem using a multiplication fact.

The teacher has 5 tubs and puts 6 brushes in each tub.
How many brushes altogether?

___ × ___ = ___

Jane cut 2 pizzas into quarters. How many slices altogether?

___ × ___ = ___

There are 5 octopuses in the tank. How many legs altogether?

___ × ___ = ___

There are 3 crabs in the tank. How many legs altogether?

___ × ___ = ___

Clare and Jake have 9 felt pens each. How many pens altogether?

___ × ___ = ___

There are 3 vases and each one is empty. How many flowers altogether?

___ × ___ = ___

Jake has 2 blue boxes and 3 red boxes. He has put 10 cars in each box.
How many cars altogether?

___ × ___ = ___

Clare ate 6 lollies. Jake ate double that amount.
How many lollies did Jake eat?

___ × ___ = ___

BOB time!

MULTIPLYING by 4

Look at the 4 times table below. You should already know the ones in red that use the **0s**, **1s**, **2s**, **5s** and **10s** multiplication facts because you know the **turnarounds**.

4 × 0 = 0	**0 × any number = 0**
4 × 1 = 4	**1 × 4 = 4**
4 × 2 = 8	**2 × 4 = 8**
4 × 3 = 12	
4 × 4 = 16	
4 × 5 = 20	**5 × 4 = 20**
4 × 6 = 24	
4 × 7 = 28	
4 × 8 = 32	
4 × 9 = 36	
4 × 10 = 40	**10 × 4 = 40**

You already know that **2 × 4** or **double 4** equals **8**. To find **4 × 4**, you can **double 4** to get **8** and then **double 8** to get **16**. This diagram might help you understand this better.

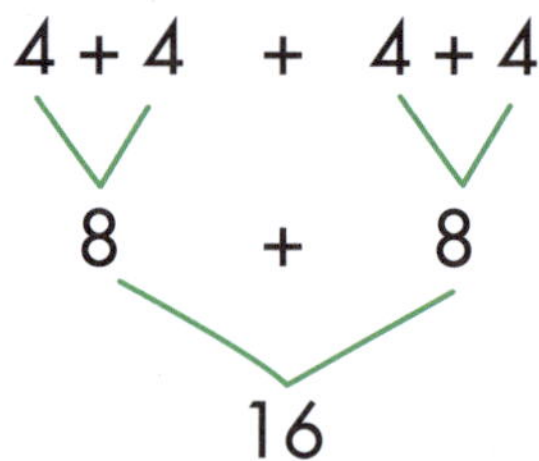

This works for all of the 4s multiplication facts.

Show the double double steps for working out 4 × 3 and complete the multiplication fact.

3 + 3 + 3 + 3

6 + 6

12

4 × 3 = 12

We practise

Circle which strategies you could use to answer this multiplication fact:

4 × 5

1s fact	10s facts
2s fact	double double
5s fact	turnaround

Complete the multiplication fact.

4 × 5 = 20

Back to Basics™

MULTIPLICATION TABLES

YEARS 2 and 3

Back to Basics™
MULTIPLICATION TABLES
YEARS 2 and 3

Back to Basics™
MULTIPLICATION TABLES
YEARS 2 and 3

Back to Basics™
MULTIPLICATION TABLES
YEARS 2 and 3

Back to Basics™
MULTIPLICATION TABLES
YEARS 2 and 3

Back to Basics™
MULTIPLICATION TABLES
YEARS 2 and 3

Back to Basics™
MULTIPLICATION TABLES
YEARS 2 and 3

Back to Basics™
MULTIPLICATION TABLES
YEARS 2 and 3

Back to Basics™
MULTIPLICATION TABLES
YEARS 2 and 3

Back to Basics™
MULTIPLICATION TABLES
YEARS 2 and 3

Back to Basics™
MULTIPLICATION TABLES
YEARS 2 and 3

Back to Basics™
MULTIPLICATION TABLES
YEARS 2 and 3

Back to Basics™
MULTIPLICATION TABLES
YEARS 2 and 3

Back to Basics™
MULTIPLICATION TABLES
YEARS 2 and 3

Back to Basics™
MULTIPLICATION TABLES
YEARS 2 and 3

Back to Basics™
MULTIPLICATION TABLES
YEARS 2 and 3

0	1	2	3
4	5	6	7
8	9	0	1
2	3	4	5

6	7	8	9
0	2	3	4
5	2	3	4
5	0	7	9

Back to Basics

MULTIPLICATION TABLES

YEARS 2 and 3

Back to Basics
MULTIPLICATION TABLES
YEARS 2 and 3
Back to Basics
MULTIPLICATION TABLES
YEARS 2 and 3
Back to Basics
MULTIPLICATION TABLES
YEARS 2 and 3
Back to Basics
MULTIPLICATION TABLES
YEARS 2 and 3
Back to Basics
MULTIPLICATION TABLES
YEARS 2 and 3
Back to Basics
MULTIPLICATION TABLES
YEARS 2 and 3
Back to Basics
MULTIPLICATION TABLES
YEARS 2 and 3
Back to Basics
MULTIPLICATION TABLES
YEARS 2 and 3
Back to Basics
MULTIPLICATION TABLES
YEARS 2 and 3
Back to Basics
MULTIPLICATION TABLES
YEARS 2 and 3
Back to Basics
MULTIPLICATION TABLES
YEARS 2 and 3
Back to Basics
MULTIPLICATION TABLES
YEARS 2 and 3
Back to Basics
MULTIPLICATION TABLES
YEARS 2 and 3
Back to Basics
MULTIPLICATION TABLES
YEARS 2 and 3
Back to Basics
MULTIPLICATION TABLES
YEARS 2 and 3

You practise

Show the double double steps for working out each multiplication fact.

1 4×4

___ + ___ + ___ + ___

___ + ___

___

3 4×9

___ + ___ + ___ + ___

___ + ___

___

2 4×6

___ + ___ + ___ + ___

___ + ___

___

4 4×7

___ + ___ + ___ + ___

___ + ___

___

You practise

Which strategy could you use for each multiplication? Complete each multiplication fact.

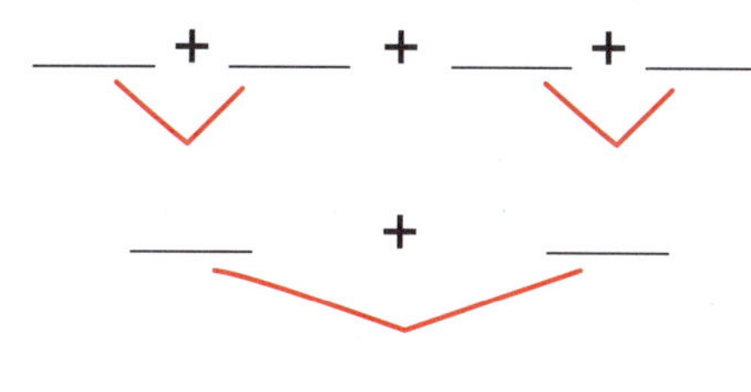

Strategies:
5s fact   10s fact   double double   double

5 $4 \times 2 =$ ___ ___________

6 $4 \times 6 =$ ___ ___________

7 $4 \times 5 =$ ___ ___________

8 $4 \times 10 =$ ___ ___________

LET'S GET SPEEDY

This game is a good way to practise your multiplication facts and strategies.

Play this game with two other people. To start, one person calls out a fact from the chart below and then the other two players shout the answer as fast as they can. The first player to shout the correct answer wins the round.

×	0	1	2	3	4	5	6	7	8	9	10
0	0	0	0	0	0	0	0	0	0	0	0
1	0	1	2	3	4	5	6	7	8	9	10
2	0	2	4	6	8	10	12	14	16	18	20
4	0	4	8	12	16	20	24	28	32	36	40
5	0	5	10	15	20	25	30	35	40	45	50
10	0	10	20	30	40	50	60	70	80	90	100

Colour the numbers that are in the 2s facts green and the numbers that are in the 5s facts black to find the hidden picture.

7	3	11	17	19	9	3	7	1
11	1	2	6	14	12	18	2	9
13	12	8	16	18	4	8	12	3
3	14	15	8	4	6	5	16	17
17	19	3	7	1	11	17	9	3

Work out these multiplication facts as fast as you can. Circle any that you were slow at or didn't know.

3 × 5 = 15

2 × 7 = 14

7 × 4 = 28

6 × 2 = 12

7 × 0 = 0

We practise

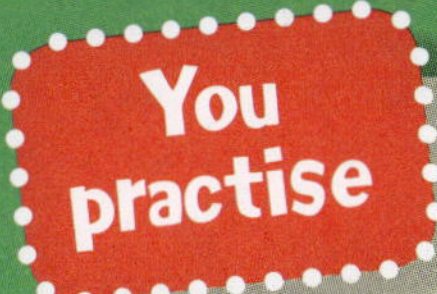

Colour the numbers as directed to find the hidden picture.

Colour the numbers that are in the 2s facts red, the numbers that are in the 5s facts yellow and all the other numbers green.

9	17	13	21	11	27	29
1	19	23	2	25	33	3
3	7	4	4	6	1	7
11	12	16	22	14	18	9
13	5	25	45	35	45	17
19	25	15	16	15	55	29
21	35	35	4	50	15	31
27	15	25	18	35	45	9
19	13	9	7	1	3	7

If you get stuck, look at the **multiplication chart** on the opposite page, or better still, try to think of a **strategy** to help you get unstuck.

You practise

Say out loud the answers to each multiplication fact. Ask someone to time you.

 5 × 4 =

 3 × 1 =

 10 × 10 =

 2 × 8 =

 8 × 0 =

 5 × 7 =

 7 × 2 =

 5 × 9 =

 1 × 9 =

 3 × 5 =

Learn the ones that you were slow at and then do the test again. Did you improve? **Keep trying!**

BOB time!

SKIP COUNTING in 3s

Being able to count in 3s helps with learning the 3 times table.

Every third number is **red** in this counting sequence. These are the numbers in the **3s counting sequence**.

1	2	3	4	5	6	7	8	9	10
11	12	13	14	15	16	17	18	19	20
21	22	23	24	25	26	27	28	29	30

Read the **red** numbers as fast as you can. Do it again and again, faster and faster, until you remember them.

Say them in funny voices or backwards.

You can make your **calculator** into a **count-by-3s machine** by pressing these keys:

Can you say the numbers at the same time as the calculator display? If you practise enough you will be able to.

We practise

Complete the counting-by-3s sequence.

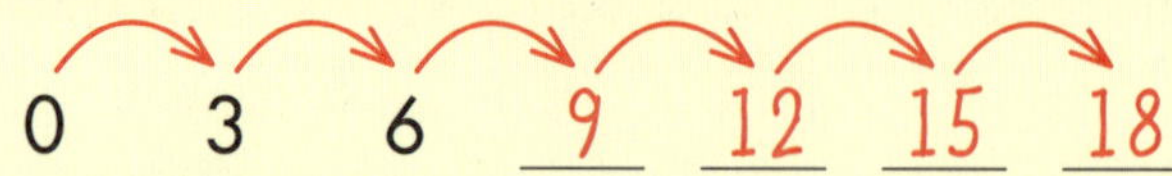

How many jumps of 3 are needed to get from start to finish?

6

Complete the counting sequence to find the starting number and the finishing number.

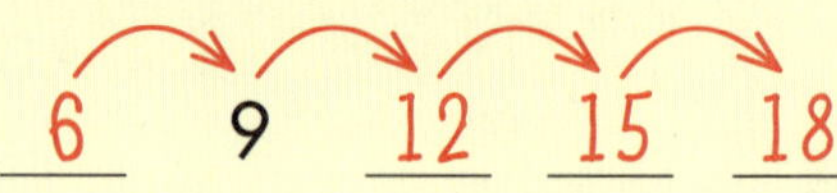

You practise

Complete each counting-by-3s sequence. How many jumps of 3 are needed to get from start to finish?

1. 0 3 6 ___ ___

___ jumps

2. 0 3 6 ___ ___ ___

___ jumps

3. 0 3 6 9 ___ ___ ___ ___ ___

___ jumps

4. 0 3 6 ___ ___ ___ ___

___ jumps

5. 30 27 ___ ___ ___ ___ ___

___ jumps

Use the **counting-by-3s sequence** on the opposite page if you need to.

You practise

Complete each counting-by-3s sequence.

6. ___ 9 12 ___ ___

7. ___ ___ 9 12 ___ ___ ___

8. ___ ___ 15 18 ___ ___

9. ___ ___ ___ 21 ___ ___

10. ___ 24 21 ___ ___ ___ ___

BOB time!

3s MULTIPLICATION FACTS

Look at the 3s multiplication facts below.

You already know about **turnarounds**, **doubles** and **double doubles**. You also know the **1s**, **2s**, **4s**, **5s** and **10s** multiplication facts.

So you already know:

3 × 1 = 3	1 × 3 = 3	turnaround
3 × 2 = 6	2 × 3 = 6	turnaround and double 3 + 3 = 6
3 × 4 = 12	4 × 3 = 12	turnaround and double double (3 + 3 + 3 + 3 = 6 + 6 = 12)
3 × 5 = 15	5 × 3 = 15	turnaround

You already know strategies that will make learning the 3s facts really easy.

An array is simply a collection of things. 3 × 3 is called a square number because it makes a square array.

One strategy that helps with 3 × 3 is to think about it as a **square array** (or **square number**), as shown here.

To get really fast with 3s facts you can play beat the calculator with a partner. Try to answer any of the 3s multiplication facts before your partner has time to get the answer on the calculator.

What strategy helps you complete this multiplication fact? What is the answer?

3 × 5

Strategy: Turnaround
5 x 3 = 15

Circle the two facts that match.

3 × 4 = 12

4 + 4 + 4 = 12

2 × 6 = 12

You practise What strategy or strategies help you complete each multiplication fact? What is the answer?

Strategy ______

3 × 1 = ___

Strategy ______

3 × 4 = ___

Strategy ______

3 × 5 = ___

Strategy ______

3 × 3 = ___

Remember turnarounds, doubles and double doubles, and 1s, 2s, 4s, 5s and 10s multiplication facts.

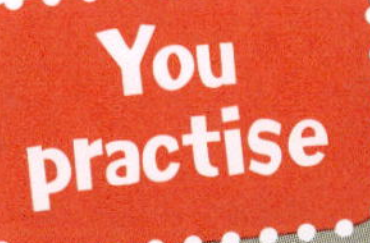

Complete each fact and circle the two facts that match in each row.

3 × 2 = ___ 2 + 2 + 2 = ___ double 2 = ___

3 × 3 = ___ 6 × 3 = ___ 3 + 3 + 3 = ___

3 × 5 = ___ 5 × 3 = ___ 3 + 3 + 3 + 3 = ___

3 × 1 = ___ 3 + 1 = ___ 1 + 1 + 1 = ___

BOB time!

MORE 3s MULTIPLICATION FACTS

Only **five** more **3s facts** to learn!
Here are some **strategies** to help you.

3 × 6 = 18

You know **3 × 3 = 9** and 3 × 6 is **twice** as much as **3 × 3**, so **double 9 = 18**.

Look at the diagram below to help you understand this.

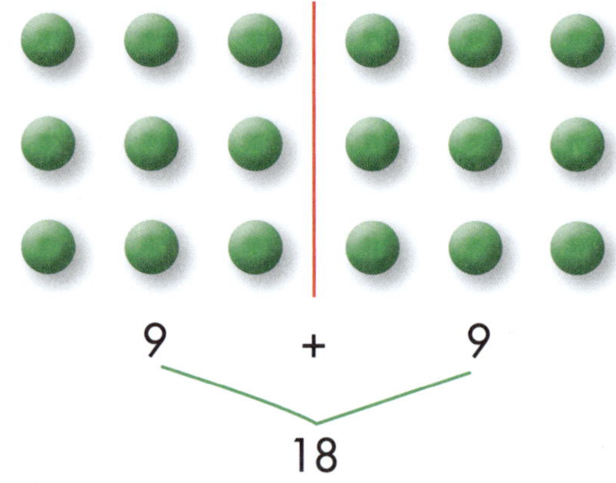

9 + 9 → 18

3 × 7 = 21

You know **double 7 = 14**, so quickly **add 7 more** to make **21**.

7 + 7 + 7
14
21

3 × 8 = 24

You know **double 8 = 16**, so quickly **add 8 more** to make **24**.

8 + 8 + 8
16
24

3 × 9 = 27

You know the **close fact 3 × 10 = 30**, so **take away 3** to make **27**.

3 × 10 = 30

You know the **turnaround 10 × 3 = 30** from the **10s facts**.

What strategy will help you find 3 × 8?

Strategy: Double 8 = 16, then add 8 more to make 24

3 × 8 = 24

Complete these multiplication facts.

3 × 7 = 21

3 × 6 = 18

3 × 9 = 27

You practise What strategy that you already know about will help you answer these multiplication facts?

Strategy ______________________

$3 \times 6 =$ ____

Strategy ______________________

$3 \times 9 =$ ____

Strategy ______________________

$3 \times 7 =$ ____

Strategy ______________________

$3 \times 8 =$ ____

You practise Complete these multiplication facts.

5. $3 \times 7 =$ ____

6. ____ $\times 8 = 24$

7. $3 \times$ ____ $= 27$

8. $3 \times$ ____ $= 24$

9. $3 \times$ ____ $= 30$

10. $7 \times$ ____ $= 21$

How did you go? Do you need to do a bit more practise?

BOB time!

MULTIPLICATION and DIVISION

When you share a group of things into smaller, equal-sized groups you are dividing or doing division.

Look at the **division sign** in this fact:

8 ÷ 2

You can use the **multiplication fact 2 × 4 = 8** (or **double 4 = 8**) to help with this division.

To divide by **2**, ask yourself: **what is half of 8**? This is the **opposite of doubling**.

This diagram shows how to divide 8 counters in half.

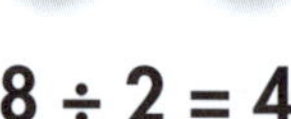

This is written as: **8 ÷ 2 = 4**

For **8 ÷ 4**, you can divide the 8 counters into **4** groups and then count how many in each group.

This is written as: **8 ÷ 4 = 2**

These multiplication and division facts are all related.

4 × 2 = 8	**8 ÷ 4 = 2**
2 × 4 = 8	**8 ÷ 2 = 4**

We practise

Which multiplication fact helps with 10 ÷ 2?

2 × 5 = 10

What is the answer?

10 ÷ 2 = 5

Write the multiplication fact and the division fact to show 12 marbles shared into 6 groups.

2 × 6 = 12

12 ÷ 6 = 2

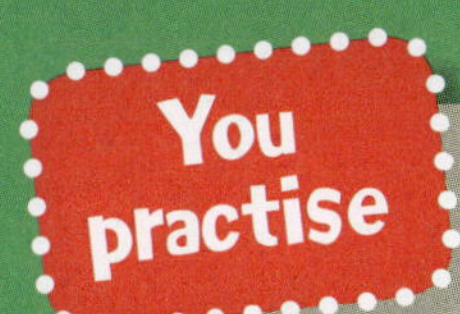

Which multiplication fact helps with each division question? What is the answer?

___ × ___ = ___   6 ÷ 2 = ___

___ × ___ = ___   16 ÷ 2 = ___

___ × ___ = ___   14 ÷ 2 = ___

You practise

Write the multiplication fact and division fact for each question.

12 marbles are put into bags of 2.
How many bags are there?

___ × ___ = ___   ___ ÷ ___ = ___

12 marbles are shared between 2 children.
How many marbles does each child have?

___ × ___ = ___   ___ ÷ ___ = ___

16 pens are put into 2 packets.
How many pens are in each packet?

___ × ___ = ___   ___ ÷ ___ = ___

BOB time!

MORE DIVISION FACTS

You should now know all the multiplication facts in this chart.

×	0	1	2	3	4	5	6	7	8	9	10
0	0	0	0	0	0	0	0	0	0	0	0
1	0	1	2	3	4	5	6	7	8	9	10
2	0	2	4	6	8	10	12	14	16	18	20
3	0	3	6	9	12	15	18	21	24	27	30
4	0	4	8	12	16	20	24	28	32	36	40
5	0	5	10	15	20	25	30	35	40	45	50
10	0	10	20	30	40	50	60	70	80	90	100

You can also use this chart to find answers to **division** questions.

To find **12 ÷ 3**, put your finger on **3** in the first column, then slide it along the row until you find **12**. Then slide it up the column to the top row to **4**. This tells you that:

12 ÷ 3 = 4

Try **12 ÷ 4**. Put your finger on **4** in the first column, then slide it along the row until you come to **12**, then slide it up to the top row to **3**. This tells you that:

12 ÷ 4 = 3

Notice that both **12 ÷ 3 = 4** and **12 ÷ 4 = 3** relate to the multiplication facts **3 × 4 = 12** and **4 × 3= 12**.

Use the chart to find the answer to:

25 ÷ 5 = 5

Use the chart to find the related multiplication fact for 24 ÷ 4.

4 × 6 = 24

You practise

Answer these division questions.

24 ÷ 4 = ___

35 ÷ 5 = ___

18 ÷ 3 = ___

36 ÷ 4 = ___

45 ÷ 5 = ___

6 27 ÷ 3 = ___

7 28 ÷ 4 = ___

8 16 ÷ 4 = ___

9 21 ÷ 3 = ___

30 ÷ 10 = ___

Use the **multiplication chart** on the opposite page if you need to.

What is your personal best? ___ seconds

What is the related multiplication fact for each of these division questions?

28 ÷ 4 = ___ ___ × ___ = ___

45 ÷ 5 = ___ ___ × ___ = ___

18 ÷ 2 = ___ ___ × ___ = ___

18 ÷ 3 = ___ ___ × ___ = ___

32 ÷ 4 = ___ ___ × ___ = ___

Remember to use the **multiplication chart** if you need to.

LET'S GET SPEEDY with MULTIPLICATION

Now it's time to check which **multiplication facts** you are really speedy with and which ones you need to **practise**.

Look at the multiplication tables. Recite each fact and then shade the ones that you know. This will tell you which ones you need to learn.

0 facts	1 facts	2 facts
0 × 0 = 0	1 × 0 = 0	2 × 0 = 0
0 × 1 = 0	1 × 1 = 1	2 × 1 = 2
0 × 2 = 0	1 × 2 = 2	2 × 2 = 4
0 × 3 = 0	1 × 3 = 3	2 × 3 = 6
0 × 4 = 0	1 × 4 = 4	2 × 4 = 8
0 × 5 = 0	1 × 5 = 5	2 × 5 = 10
0 × 6 = 0	1 × 6 = 6	2 × 6 = 12
0 × 7 = 0	1 × 7 = 7	2 × 7 = 14
0 × 8 = 0	1 × 8 = 8	2 × 8 = 16
0 × 9 = 0	1 × 9 = 9	2 × 9 = 18
0 × 10 = 0	1 × 10 = 10	2 × 10 = 20

When you feel confident, play beat the calculator with a partner. Your partner calls out the facts that you haven't shaded and then you try to answer before your partner has time to get the answer on the calculator.

3 facts	4 facts	5 facts	10 facts
3 × 0 = 0	4 × 0 = 0	5 × 0 = 0	10 × 0 = 0
3 × 1 = 3	4 × 1 = 4	5 × 1 = 5	10 × 1 = 10
3 × 2 = 6	4 × 2 = 8	5 × 2 = 10	10 × 2 = 20
3 × 3 = 9	4 × 3 = 12	5 × 3 = 15	10 × 3 = 30
3 × 4 = 12	4 × 4 = 16	5 × 4 = 20	10 × 4 = 40
3 × 5 = 15	4 × 5 = 20	5 × 5 = 25	10 × 5 = 50
3 × 6 = 18	4 × 6 = 24	5 × 6 = 30	10 × 6 = 60
3 × 7 = 21	4 × 7 = 28	5 × 7 = 35	10 × 7 = 70
3 × 8 = 24	4 × 8 = 32	5 × 8 = 40	10 × 8 = 80
3 × 9 = 27	4 × 9 = 36	5 × 9 = 45	10 × 9 = 90
3 × 10 = 30	4 × 10 = 40	5 × 10 = 50	10 × 10 = 100

Answer these multiplication questions.

2 × 2 = 4 3 × 1 = 3

1 × 7 = 7 7 × 1 = 7

5 × 0 = 0

We practise

Which multiplication facts have the answer 12?

2 × 6 6 × 2

3 × 4 4 × 3

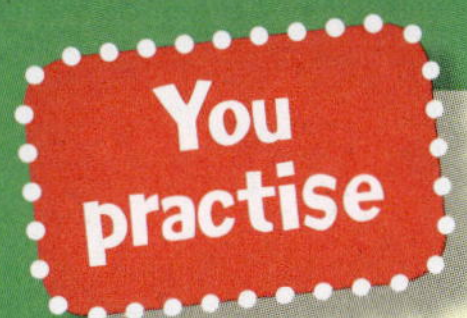

Speed Test: Ask a partner to time you as you write the answers to these multiplication facts.

0 facts	1 facts	2 facts
0 × 0 = ____	1 × 0 = ____	2 × 0 = ____
0 × 1 = ____	1 × 1 = ____	2 × 1 = ____
0 × 2 = ____	1 × 2 = ____	2 × 2 = ____
0 × 3 = ____	1 × 3 = ____	2 × 3 = ____
0 × 4 = ____	1 × 4 = ____	2 × 4 = ____
0 × 5 = ____	1 × 5 = ____	2 × 5 = ____
0 × 6 = ____	1 × 6 = ____	2 × 6 = ____
0 × 7 = ____	1 × 7 = ____	2 × 7 = ____
0 × 8 = ____	1 × 8 = ____	2 × 8 = ____
0 × 9 = ____	1 × 9 = ____	2 × 9 = ____
0 × 10 = ____	1 × 10 = ____	2 × 10 = ____

You can also use the **multiplication chart** for **division**.

3 facts	4 facts	5 facts	10 facts
3 × 0 = ____	4 × 0 = ____	5 × 0 = ____	10 × 0 = ____
3 × 1 = ____	4 × 1 = ____	5 × 1 = ____	10 × 1 = ____
3 × 2 = ____	4 × 2 = ____	5 × 2 = ____	10 × 2 = ____
3 × 3 = ____	4 × 3 = ____	5 × 3 = ____	10 × 3 = ____
3 × 4 = ____	4 × 4 = ____	5 × 4 = ____	10 × 4 = ____
3 × 5 = ____	4 × 5 = ____	5 × 5 = ____	10 × 5 = ____
3 × 6 = ____	4 × 6 = ____	5 × 6 = ____	10 × 6 = ____
3 × 7 = ____	4 × 7 = ____	5 × 7 = ____	10 × 7 = ____
3 × 8 = ____	4 × 8 = ____	5 × 8 = ____	10 × 8 = ____
3 × 9 = ____	4 × 9 = ____	5 × 9 = ____	10 × 9 = ____
3 × 10 = ____	4 × 10 = ____	5 × 10 = ____	10 × 10 = ____

BOB time!

LET'S GET SPEEDY with DIVISION

Close your eyes and randomly put your finger somewhere in the middle of this chart. Look at the number.

Without using the chart, make two division facts with this number as the answer. For example, if you point to **15**, the two division facts are **15 ÷ 3 = 5** and **15 ÷ 5 = 3**.

×	0	1	2	3	4	5	6	7	8	9	10
0	0	0	0	0	0	0	0	0	0	0	0
1	0	1	2	3	4	5	6	7	8	9	10
2	0	2	4	6	8	10	12	14	16	18	20
4	0	4	8	12	16	20	24	28	32	36	40
5	0	5	10	15	20	25	30	35	40	45	50
10	0	10	20	30	40	50	60	70	80	90	100

You can also use the **multiplication chart** for **division.**

Play beat the calculator with a partner.

Your partner calls out a division fact from the chart and then you try to answer before your partner has time to get the answer on the calculator.

We practise

Fill in the missing × or ÷ signs and missing numbers to find the middle number. Start in the left corner and wind your way around to the middle.

3	×	4	=	12
=	5	×	3	÷
2	=	5	=	6
÷	3	÷	15	=
10	=	5	×	2

Remember, when you are dividing, ask yourself: **What multiplication fact can help?**

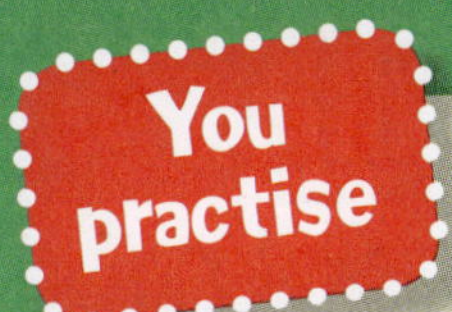

Fill in the missing × or ÷ signs and missing numbers to find the middle number.

Start in the top left corner and wind your way around to the middle.

2	÷		=	2
=	8		2	
3	=	16	=	3
	4	×		=
24	=	4		

5	×		=	10
=	4		3	÷
5	=		=	2
÷	6	÷		=
20	=		×	

BOB time!

PROBLEM SOLVING with MULTIPLICATION and DIVISION

Clare and Jake have 30 treats. Clare wants 6 treats in each bag and she has made 4 bags. Jake wants 5 treats in each bag and he has made 5 bags.

How many more bags can Clare and Jake each make?

Notice that the important information is highlighted in blue and what has to be found out is highlighted in pink.

To solve this problem, follow these steps:

Step 1 How many treats has Clare used? **4 × 6 = 24**

Step 2 How many treats has Jake used? **5 × 5 = 25**

Step 3 **Clare 30 – 24 = 6** **Jake 30 – 5 = 5**

Answer Clare has 6 treats left, which is enough for **1 more bag**.
Jake has 5 treats left, which is enough for **1 more bag**.

Remember to write the answer as a sentence.

We practise

Highlight the important information and what has to be found out and then solve the problem.

Clare had 18 lollies to share equally between herself, her brother Jake and 4 friends. How many lollies does each person get?

Step 1 How many people need to share the lollies? 6

Step 2 How many lollies does each person get? 18 ÷ 6 = 3

Answer Each person gets 3 lollies.

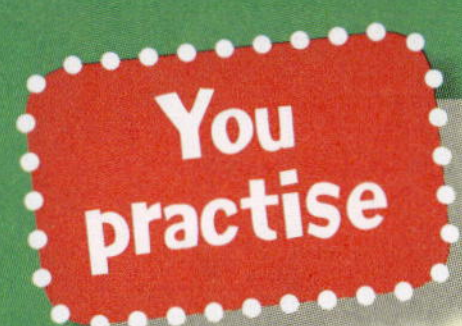

Highlight the important information and solve these problems using multiplication or division.

1. There are 4 tubs with 7 red pens in each and 3 tubs with 8 blue pens in each. How many more red than blue pens are there?

2. Jake has sorted his 28 toy cars into 4 groups. How many cars in each group?

3. There are 24 pens. What are two ways that these pens can be shared equally?

4. Clare sorted her 32 collector cards into groups of 4. How many cards in each group?

5. Mrs Brown's hens have laid 4 eggs every day this week. How many eggs are there?

   How many egg cartons are needed for the eggs?

6. Jake says there are 4 ways of making a 12 by multiplying two numbers together. What are they?

7. Mum has baked 24 cookies. She wants to make 3 packets with 4 cookies in each and the rest put into packets of 3. How many packets of 3 can she make?

8. At the end of the game of beanbag toss, Clare had scored three 6s and three 5s. Jake had scored four 7s and two 4s. Who won and by how much?

9. The teacher has some counters in her hand. The number of counters is in both the 5s and 10s counting sequences. You can make 4 or 5 equal-sized groups with the counters. How many counters are there?

10. Jake poured 4 bags of 6 counters into a tub and then shared them equally into 3 bags. How many counters in each bag?

BOB time!

TEST 1

Complete this counting sequence.

6 8 ___ ___ ___ ___ ___ 20

Divide these counters into groups of 2s and write the matching multiplication fact.

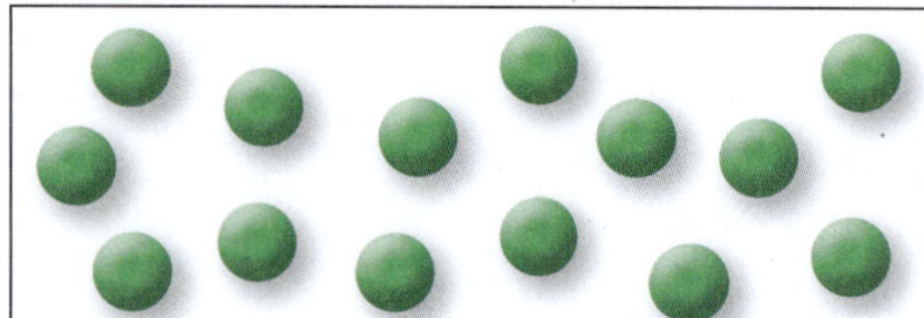

____

Write the double fact and the multiplication fact for this group of counters.

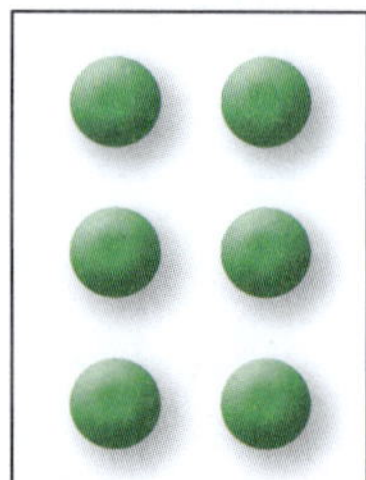

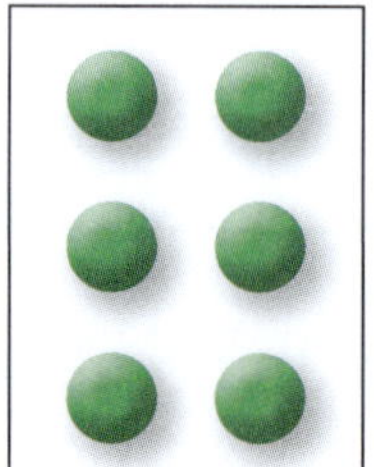

____

____

Divide these counters into groups of 5 and write the matching multiplication fact.

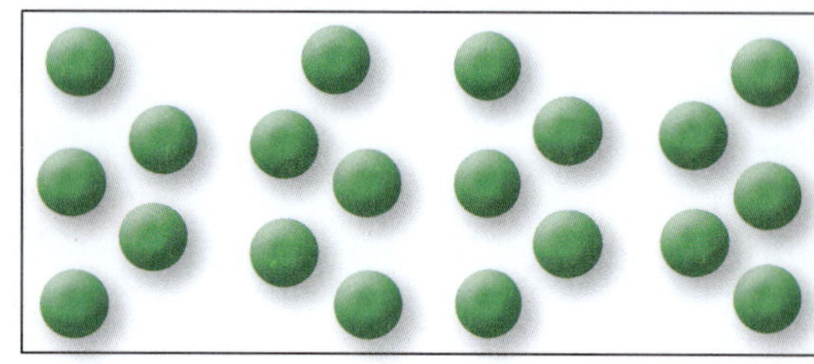

____

Complete the multiplication fact and write its turnaround fact.

6 × 5 = ______

____

Complete the multiplication fact and write its turnaround fact.

2 × 9 = ____

____

Circle the number that is in the 5s counting sequence. Write the matching multiplication fact.

36 25 32 51

____

Circle the number that is in the 5s counting sequence. Write the matching multiplication fact.

43 32 60 38

____

Circle the answer to the multiplication fact 6 × 1.

6 7 8

6 × 0 = ____

TEST 2

Complete these multiplication facts.

4 × 4 = ____

4 × 7 = ____

4 × 8 = ____

Complete this count-in-3s sequence.

___ ___ 15 18 ___ ___ ___

If you have 3 bags of 7 marbles, how many marbles are there altogether?

____ marbles

Which multiplication fact is useful for working out 3 × 9?

____

Complete these multiplication facts.

0 × 7 = ____

6 × 0 = ____

4 × 1 = ____

Complete these multiplication facts.

3 × 9 = ____

4 × 7 = ____

3 × 7 = ____

Complete these division facts.

6 ÷ 2 = ____

14 ÷ 2 = ____

18 ÷ 2 = ____

If 15 marbles are shared between 3 children, how many marbles does each child get?

____ marbles

Complete these division facts.

24 ÷ 4 = ____

21 ÷ 3 = ____

30 ÷ 5 = ____

Clare made 5 bags with 5 buttons in each bag. Then she lost 4 buttons, so she made them into 3 equal bags. How many buttons in each bag now?

____ buttons

ANSWERS

Unit 1

1 6 8 10 12
6 jumps

2 8 10 12 14
7 jumps

3 12 14 16 18 20 22
11 jumps

4 14 12 10 8 6 4 2 0
10 jumps

5 2 4 6 8 10 12

6 4 6 8 10 12 14 16

7 4 6 8 10 12 14 16 18

8 12 14 16 18 20 22 24 26

Unit 2

1
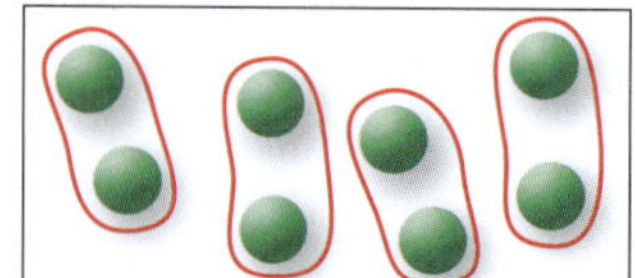
$4 \times 2 = 8$

2
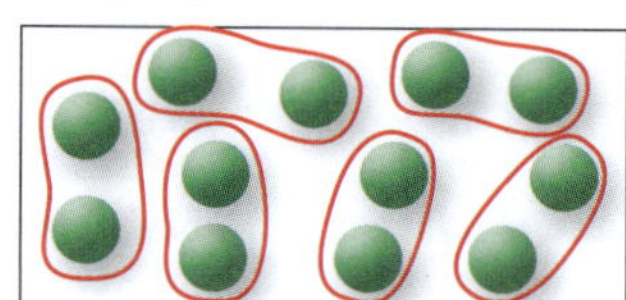
$6 \times 2 = 12$

3
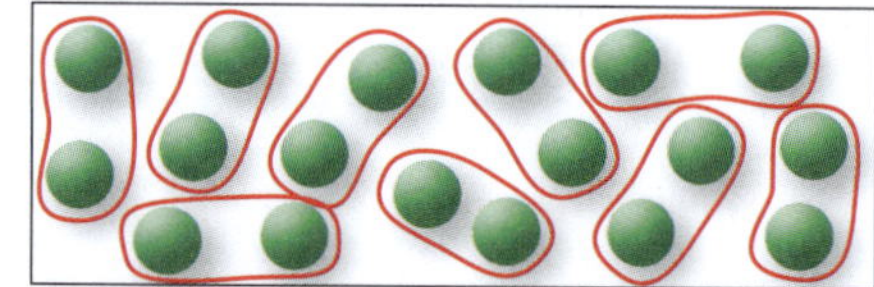
$9 \times 2 = 18$

4
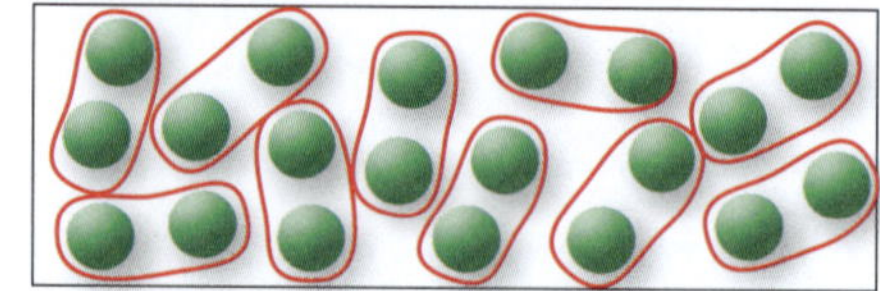
$10 \times 2 = 20$

5
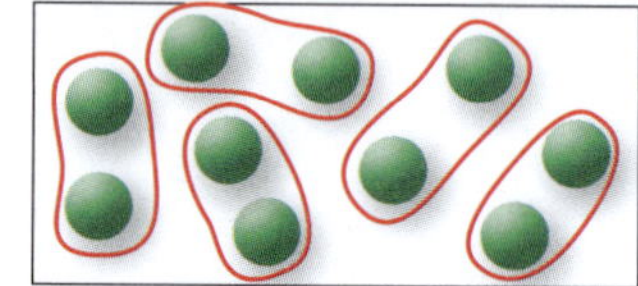
$5 \times 2 = 10$

6

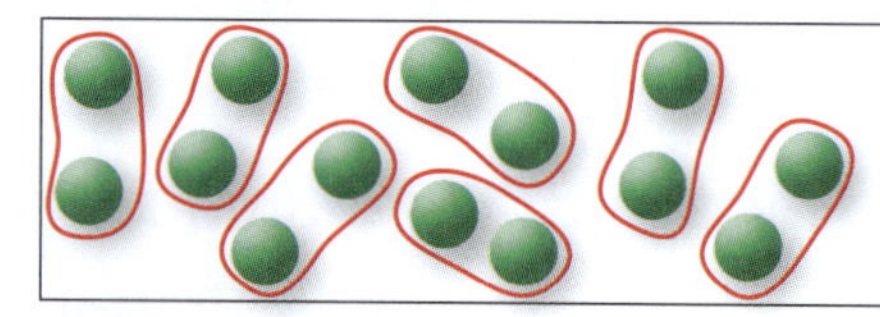
$7 \times 2 = 14$

7
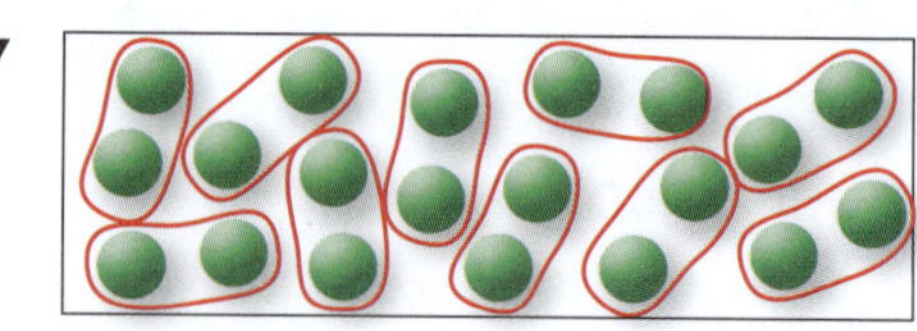
$10 \times 2 = 20$

8
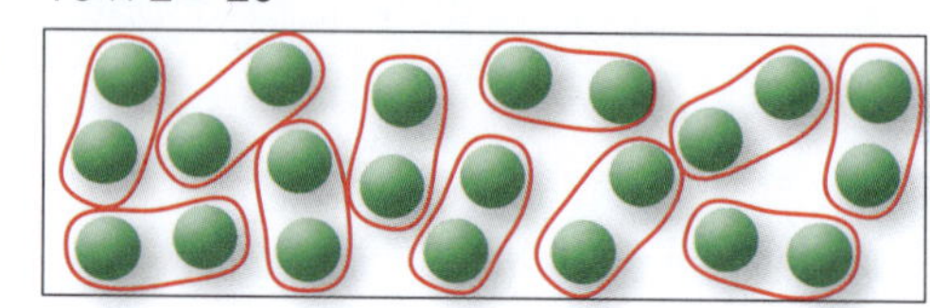
$11 \times 2 = 22$

Unit 3

1	Double 2 is 4	$2 \times 2 = 4$
2	Double 3 is 6	$2 \times 3 = 6$
3	Double 5 is 10	$2 \times 5 = 10$
4	Double 3 is 6	$2 \times 3 = 6$
	Double 6 is 12	$6 \times 2 = 12$
5	Double 5 is 10	$2 \times 5 = 10$
	Double 10 is 20	$10 \times 2 = 20$
6	Double 2 is 4	$2 \times 2 = 4$
	Double 4 is 8	$4 \times 2 = 8$

Unit 4

1 15 20 25 30
6 jumps

2 20 25 30 35
7 jumps

3 30 35 40 45 50
10 jumps

4 25 20 15 10 5 0
9 jumps

5 0 5 10 15 20

6 10 15 20 25 30 35

7 15 20 25 30 35 40

8 50 45 40 35 30 25 20 15 10

Unit 5

1
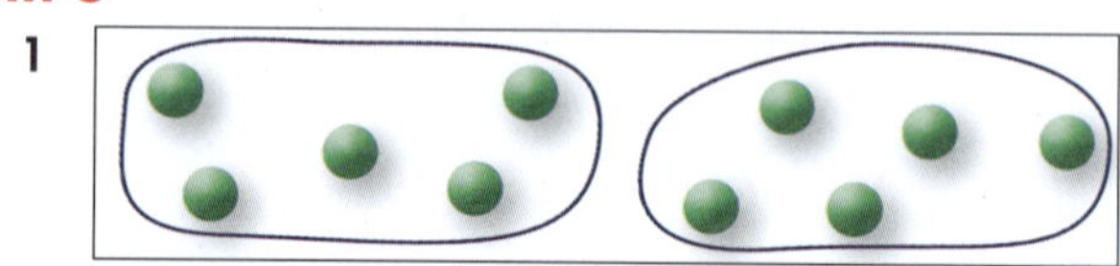
$2 \times 5 = 10$

2
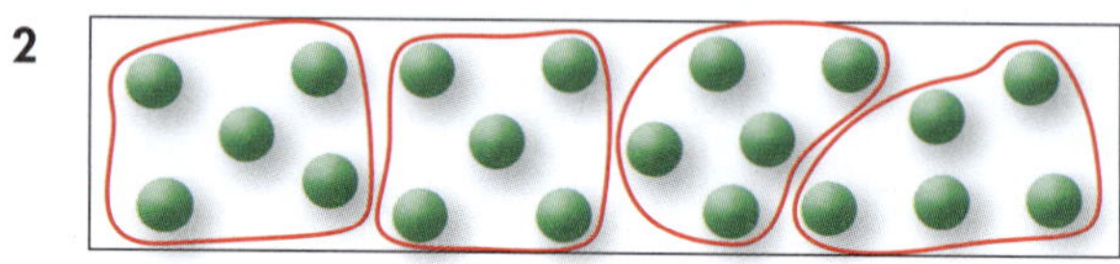
$4 \times 5 = 20$

ANSWERS

3 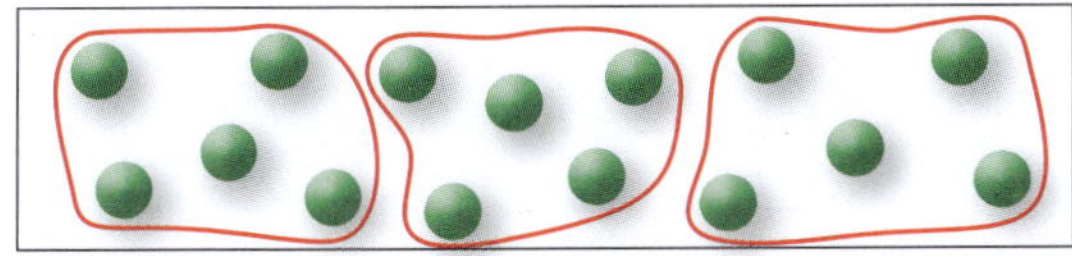

$3 \times 5 = 15$

4 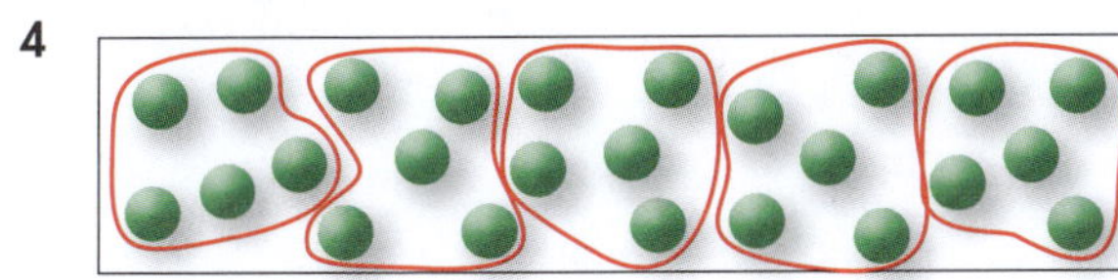

$5 \times 5 = 25$

5

$7 \times 5 = 35$

6

$6 \times 5 = 30$

7

$9 \times 5 = 45$

8

$8 \times 5 = 40$

Unit 6

1 $2 \times 6 = 12$ $6 \times 2 = 12$
2 $5 \times 4 = 20$ $4 \times 5 = 20$
3 $2 \times 7 = 14$ $7 \times 2 = 14$
4 $2 \times 9 = 18$ $9 \times 2 = 18$
5 $5 \times 6 = 30$ $6 \times 5 = 30$
6 $5 \times 4 = 20$ $4 \times 5 = 20$
7 $2 \times 4 = 8$ $4 \times 2 = 8$
8 $5 \times 10 = 50$ $10 \times 5 = 50$
9 $5 \times 7 = 35$ $7 \times 5 = 35$
10 $2 \times 9 = 18$ $9 \times 2 = 18$

Unit 7

1 40, 4 10s
2 35, 7 5s
3 50, 10 5s and 5 10s
40, 8 5s and 4 10s
4 45, 9 5s
5 $2 \times 5 = 10$ $1 \times 10 = 10$
6 $6 \times 5 = 30$ $3 \times 10 = 30$

Unit 8

1 $3 \times 1 = 3$
2 $1 \times 6 = 6$
3 $3 \times 0 = 0$
4 $0 \times 1 = 0$
5 $0 \times 6 = 0$ $3 \times 1 = 3$
4 and 6 do not belong
6 $4 \times 0 = 0$ $1 \times 7 = 7$
8 and 4 do not belong
7 $0 \times 8 = 0$ $1 \times 6 = 6$
7 and 8 do not belong
8 $9 \times 0 = 0$ $9 \times 1 = 9$
8 and 10 do not belong

Unit 9

1 $3 \times 10 = 30$
2 $2 \times 8 = 16$
3 $7 \times 5 = 35$
4 $8 \times 5 = 40$
5 $4 \times 2 = 8$
6 $5 \times 5 = 25$

Unit 10

1 $5 \times 6 = 30$
2 $2 \times 4 = 8$
3 $5 \times 8 = 40$
4 $3 \times 10 = 30$
5 $2 \times 9 = 18$
6 $3 \times 0 = 0$
7 $5 \times 10 = 50$
8 $6 \times 2 = 12$

Unit 11

1 $4 + 4 \quad + \quad 4 + 4$
$8 \quad + \quad 8$
16

2 $6 + 6 \quad + \quad 6 + 6$
$12 \quad + \quad 12$
24

3 $9 + 9 \quad + \quad 9 + 9$
$18 \quad + \quad 18$
36

4 $7 + 7 \quad + \quad 7 + 7$
$14 \quad + \quad 14$
28

5 8 double
6 24 double double
7 20 5s fact
8 40 10s fact

ANSWERS

Unit 12

1

9	17	13	21	11	27	29
1	19	23	2	25	33	3
3	7	4	4	6	1	7
11	12	16	22	14	18	9
13	5	25	45	35	45	17
19	25	15	16	15	55	29
21	35	35	4	50	15	31
27	15	25	18	35	45	9
19	13	9	7	1	3	7

2 5 × 4 = 20
3 3 × 1 = 3
4 10 × 10 = 100
5 2 × 8 = 16
6 8 × 0 = 0
7 5 × 7 = 35
8 7 × 2 = 14
9 5 × 9 = 45
10 1 × 9 = 9
11 3 × 5 = 15

Unit 13

1 9 12
4 jumps
2 9 12 15
5 jumps
3 12 15 18 21 24
8 jumps
4 9 12 15 18
6 jumps
5 24 21 18 15 12
6 jumps
6 6 9 12 15 18
7 3 6 9 12 15 18 21
8 9 12 15 18 21 24
9 12 15 18 21 24 27
10 27 24 21 18 15 12 9

Unit 14

1 Turnaround and 1s fact, 3
2 Turnaround and double double, 12
3 Turnaround and 5s fact, 15
4 Square number, 9
5 3 × 2 = 6
2 + 2 + 2 = 6
6 3 × 3 = 9
3 + 3 + 3 = 9
7 3 × 5 = 15
5 × 3 = 15
8 3 × 1 = 3
1 + 1 + 1 = 3

Unit 15

1 Double 6, 12 + 6 = 18
2 Close 10s fact 3 × 10, 3 × 9 = 27
3 Double 7, 14 + 7 = 21
4 Double 8, 16 + 8 = 24
5 3 × 7 = 21
6 3 × 8 = 24
7 3 × 9 = 27
8 3 × 8 = 24
9 3 × 10 = 30
10 7 × 3 = 21

Unit 16

1 2 × 3 = 6 6 ÷ 2 = 3
2 2 × 8 = 16 16 ÷ 2 = 8
3 2 × 7 = 14 14 ÷ 2 = 7
4 2 × 6 = 12 12 ÷ 6 = 2
5 2 × 6 = 12 12 ÷ 2 = 6
6 2 × 8 = 16 16 ÷ 2 = 8

Unit 17

1 24 ÷ 4 = 6
2 35 ÷ 5 = 7
3 18 ÷ 3 = 6
4 36 ÷ 4 = 9
5 45 ÷ 5 = 9
6 27 ÷ 3 = 9
7 28 ÷ 4 = 7
8 16 ÷ 4 = 4
9 21 ÷ 3 = 7
10 30 ÷ 10 = 3 3 × 8 = 32
11 28 ÷ 4 = 7 4 × 7 = 28
12 45 ÷ 5 = 9 5 × 9 = 45
13 18 ÷ 2 = 9 2 × 9 =18
14 18 ÷ 3 = 6 3 × 6 = 18
15 32 ÷ 4 = 8 4 × 8 = 32

Unit 18

See page 40

ANSWERS

Unit 19

1

2	÷	1	=	2
=	8	÷	2	×
3	=	16	=	3
÷	4	×	4	=
24	=	4	×	6

2

5	×	2	=	10
=	4	×	3	÷
5	=	2	=	2
÷	6	÷	12	=
20	=	4	×	5

Unit 20

1 $4 \times 7 = 28$ and $3 \times 8 = 24$
There are 4 more red pens.

2 $28 \div 4 = 7$
There are 7 cars in each group.

3 4 tubs of 6 or 3 tubs of 8

4 $32 \div 4 = 8$
There are 8 cards in each group.

5 $4 \times 7 = 28$. There are 28 eggs.
$12 \times 2 = 24$ and 4 more makes 28 eggs. 3 cartons are needed.

6 $2 \times 6 = 12$ $6 \times 2 = 12$
$3 \times 4 = 12$ $4 \times 3 = 12$

7 $3 \times 4 = 12$ and $24 - 12 = 12$
There are 12 cookies left over and
$12 \div 3 = 4$ more packets.

8 Clare: $3 \times 6 = 18$ and $3 \times 5 = 15$.
Score $18 + 15 = 33$.
Jake: $4 \times 7 = 28$ and $2 \times 4 = 8$.
Score $28 + 8 = 36$. Jake wins by 3.

9 $4 \times 5 = 20$, $2 \times 10 = 20$
She has 20 counters in her hand.

10 $4 \times 6 = 24$ and $24 \div 3 = 8$
There are 8 counters in each bag.

Test 1

1 10 12 14 16 18

2

$7 \times 2 = 14$

3 Double 6 is 12 $6 \times 2 = 12$

4

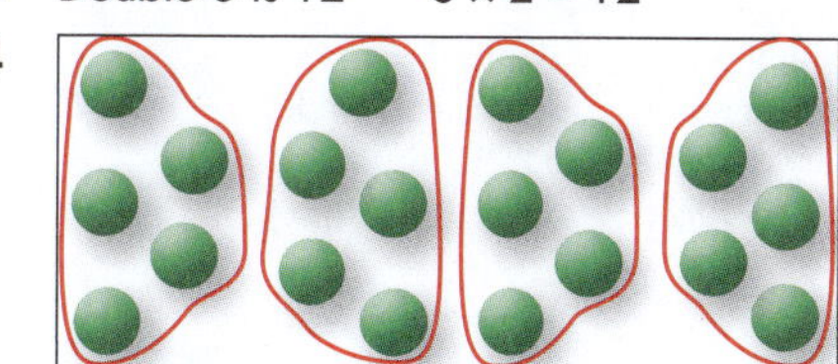

$4 \times 5 = 20$

5 $6 \times 5 = 30$ $5 \times 6 = 30$

6 $2 \times 9 = 18$ $9 \times 2 = 18$

7 25 $5 \times 5 = 25$

8 60 $10 \times 6 = 60$

9 6

10 0

Test 2

1 16 28 32

2 9 12 15 18 21 24 27

3 21

4 3×10

5 0 0 4

6 27 28 21

7 3 7 9

8 5

9 6 7 6

10 7

Back to Basics Multiplication Tables Years 2–3

Reprinted 2015, 2016, 2018, 2024

ISBN: 978 1 74215 934 8

Published by Pascal Press
PO Box 250
Glebe NSW 2037
www.pascalpress.com.au
contact@pascalpress.com.au

Author: Ann Baker
Publisher: Lynn Dickinson
Editor: Eliza Hope
Proofreader: Ruth Schultz
Design and illustration: Janice Bowles
Page layout and technical illustration: Ruth Schultz
Cover design: Deb Snibson, MAPG
Printed by Wai Man Book Binding (China) Ltd.